Rabbit or Hare?

by Christina Leaf

BLASTOFF! READERS

BELLWETHER MEDIA • MINNEAPOLIS, MN

Note to Librarians, Teachers, and Parents:

Blastoff! Readers are carefully developed by literacy experts and combine standards-based content with developmentally appropriate text.

Level 1 provides the most support through repetition of high-frequency words, light text, predictable sentence patterns, and strong visual support.

Level 2 offers early readers a bit more challenge through varied simple sentences, increased text load, and less repetition of high-frequency words.

Level 3 advances early-fluent readers toward fluency through increased text and concept load, less reliance on visuals, longer sentences, and more literary language.

Level 4 builds reading stamina by providing more text per page, increased use of punctuation, greater variation in sentence patterns, and increasingly challenging vocabulary.

Level 5 encourages children to move from "learning to read" to "reading to learn" by providing even more text, varied writing styles, and less familiar topics.

Whichever book is right for your reader, Blastoff! Readers are the perfect books to build confidence and encourage a love of reading that will last a lifetime!

This edition first published in 2020 by Bellwether Media, Inc.

No part of this publication may be reproduced in whole or in part without written permission of the publisher. For information regarding permission, write to Bellwether Media, Inc., Attention: Permissions Department, 6012 Blue Circle Drive, Minnetonka, MN 55343.

Library of Congress Cataloging-in-Publication Data

Names: Leaf, Christina, author.
Title: Rabbit or Hare? / by Christina Leaf.
Description: Minneapolis, MN : Bellwether Media, Inc., [2020] | Series: Blastoff! Readers: Spotting Differences | Includes bibliographical references and index. | Audience: Age 5-8. | Audience: K to Grade 3.
Identifiers: LCCN 2019000934 (print) | LCCN 2019001620 (ebook) |
  ISBN 9781618915764 (ebook) | ISBN 9781644870358 (hardcover : alk. paper)
Subjects: LCSH: Rabbits--Juvenile literature. | Hares--Juvenile literature.
Classification: LCC QL737.L32 (ebook) | LCC QL737.L32 L443 2020 (print) | DDC 599.32--dc23
LC record available at https://lccn.loc.gov/2019000934

Editor: Al Albertson   Designer: Jeffrey Kollock

Printed in the United States of America, North Mankato, MN.

3139303038905073

Table of Contents

Rabbits and Hares

Rabbits and hares are **mammals** that hop. Long back legs and big feet help them move.

hare

5

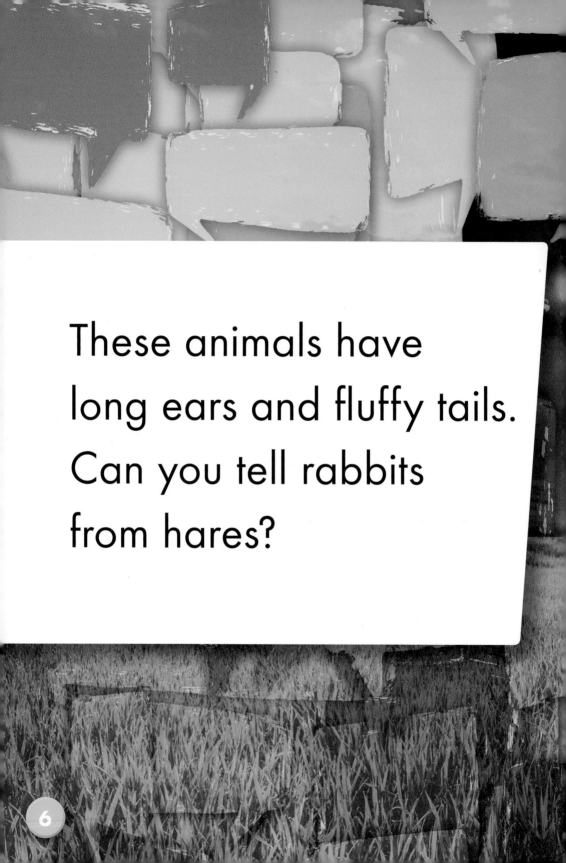

These animals have long ears and fluffy tails. Can you tell rabbits from hares?

rabbit

Different Looks

Hares have longer ears than rabbits. Their ears also have black tips.

Hares have longer legs and bigger feet, too! They run faster than rabbits.

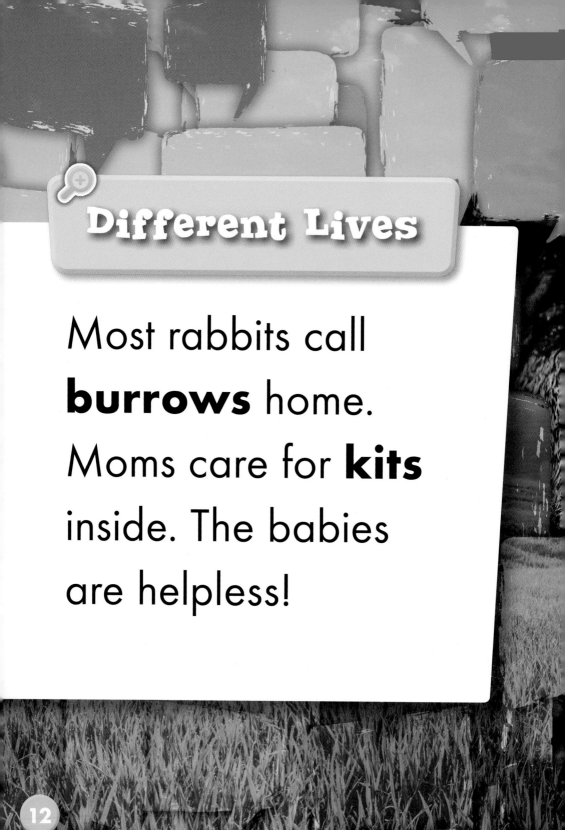

Most rabbits call **burrows** home. Moms care for **kits** inside. The babies are helpless!

kits

burrow

13

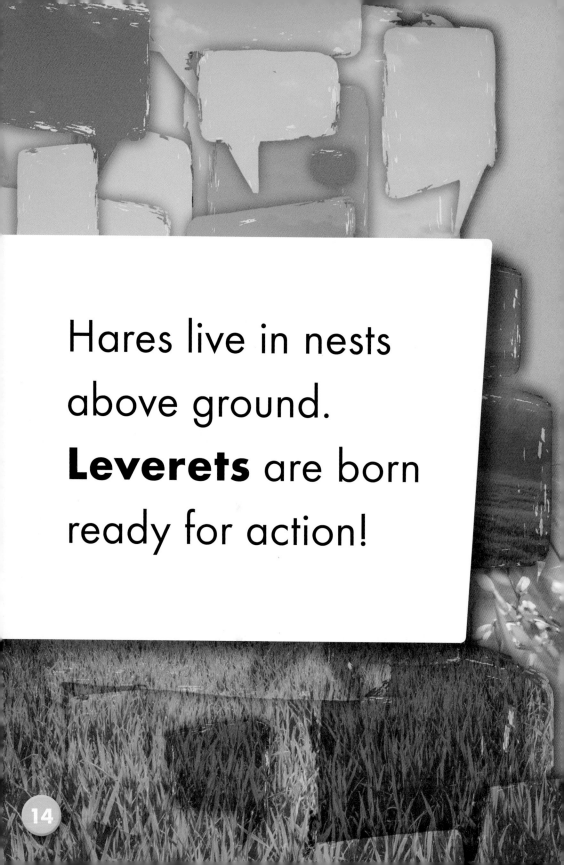

Hares live in nests above ground. **Leverets** are born ready for action!

leveret

Rabbits have many friends! They live together. Hares live alone or in pairs.

Hares run from danger. Rabbits **escape** to their burrows. Who is this safety seeker?

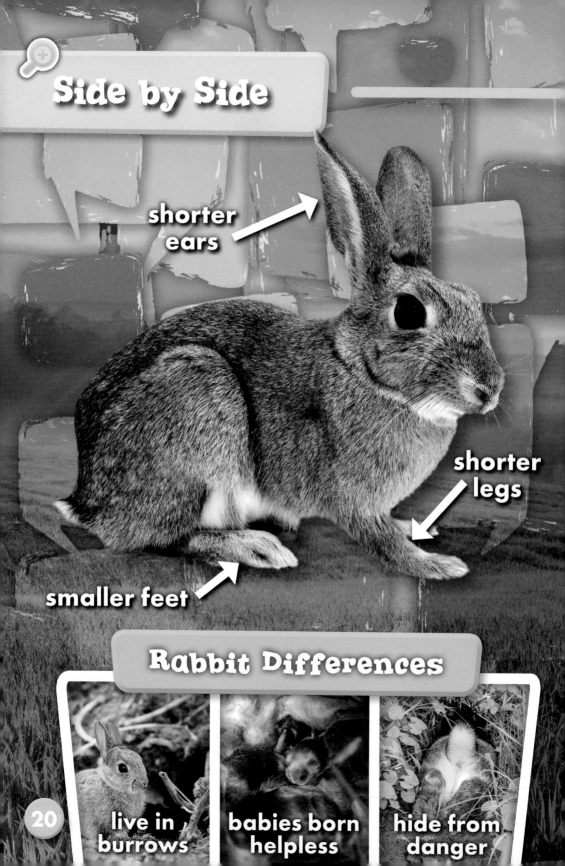

Side by Side

shorter ears

shorter legs

smaller feet

Rabbit Differences

live in burrows

babies born helpless

hide from danger

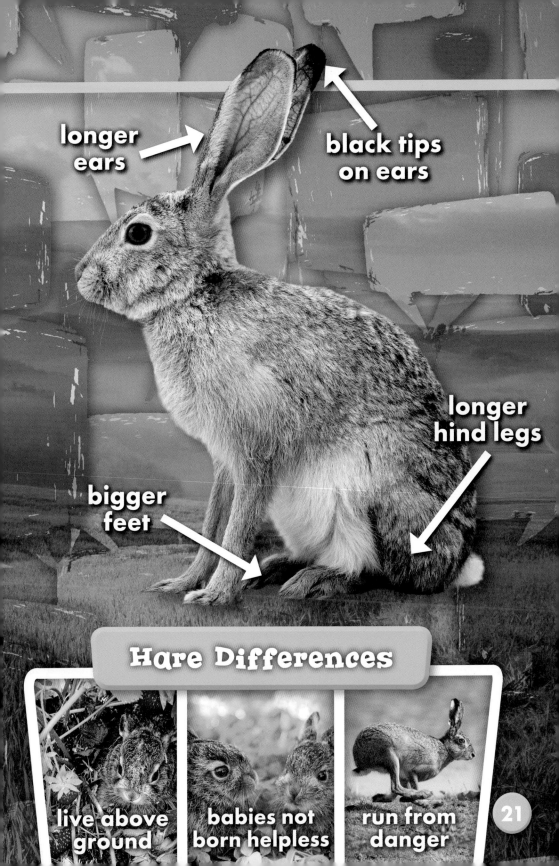

longer
ears

black tips
on ears

longer
hind legs

bigger
feet

Hare Differences

live above
ground

babies not
born helpless

run from
danger

21

Glossary

burrows

holes or tunnels in the ground some animals dig for homes

leverets

baby hares

escape

to get away

mammals

warm-blooded animals that have hair and feed their young milk

kits

baby rabbits

To Learn More

AT THE LIBRARY

Dittmer, Lori. *Rabbits*. Mankato, Minn.:
Creative Education, 2018.

Pettiford, Rebecca. *Arctic Hares*. Minneapolis,
Minn.: Bellwether Media, 2019.

Raum, Elizabeth. *Rabbits Dig Burrows*.
Mankato, Minn.: Amicus, 2018.

ON THE WEB

FACTSURFER

Factsurfer.com gives you
a safe, fun way to find
more information.

1. Go to www.factsurfer.com.

2. Enter "rabbit or hare" into the
   search box and click 🔍.

3. Select your book cover to see a list
   of related web sites.

Index